AN INTRODUCTION TO
CROP CIRCLES

edited by

ANDY THOMAS

Contents

D1354408

WESSEX BOOKS

A Member of the Independent Publishers Guild

A Modern Mystery

Standing stones pepper the Wessex landscape, including this one at Avebury.

T here is an unmistakable air of mystery that clings to ce tain counties of southern England, particularly Wiltshir once part of the ancient kingdom of Wessex. This regic has long been home to the unusual and unexplained. Believe by many to be the ancient land of King Arthur himself, th Wessex landscape embraces the Stonehenge and Avebury stor circles, the enigmatic Silbury Hill, hundreds of ancient buri mounds, scores of UFOs, mysterious black cats and dogs, ghos witches, and, most famously, crop circles.

Crop circles – corn circles, crop formations or agriglyphs, they are sometimes known – were first brought to public attentic in the 1980s, but there is clear evidence of them as far back 1678, and suggestions of others before that. Although two-thirds the world's activity occurs in England, crop circles are found a over the world. Many other countries have reported them, inclu ing Germany, Canada, The Netherlands, the Czech Republi Australia and the USA.

Circles can be found in many types of crop. Wheat and barl are the most common, but oilseed rape (canola), oats, rye, maiz flax and many other varieties have been known to host formatior Natural mediums have also been utilised by the phenomenor amongst them grassland, bracken and reputedly even tree tops. Britain, the majority of crop circles have appeared within the cou ty of Wiltshire, but other areas have also received their fair shar including Hampshire, East and West Sussex, Oxfordshir Yorkshire and even as far north as Scotland.

This book attempts to give a brief overview of the entire crc circle phenomenon – the history, the development of the patterr and the theories. While it is not intended as an exhaustive study any of the areas covered (many excellent books available for th serious researcher are listed on page 46), it will hopefully serve as starting point and whet the appetite for further study.

This design is known as a 'Julia Set' and was created at Stonehenge, Wiltshire, 7 July 1996.

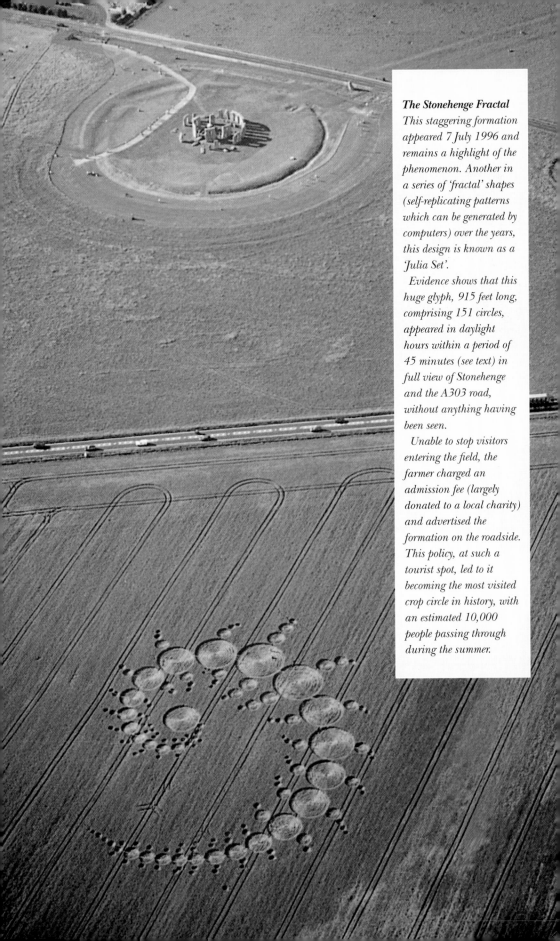

The Stonehenge Fractal
This staggering formation appeared 7 July 1996 and remains a highlight of the phenomenon. Another in a series of 'fractal' shapes (self-replicating patterns which can be generated by computers) over the years, this design is known as a 'Julia Set'.

Evidence shows that this huge glyph, 915 feet long, comprising 151 circles, appeared in daylight hours within a period of 45 minutes (see text) in full view of Stonehenge and the A303 road, without anything having been seen.

Unable to stop visitors entering the field, the farmer charged an admission fee (largely donated to a local charity) and advertised the formation on the roadside. This policy, at such a tourist spot, led to it becoming the most visited crop circle in history, with an estimated 10,000 people passing through during the summer.

A Brief History

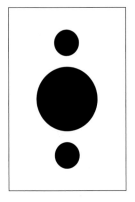

The first crop circle to gain national attention appeared at Cheesefoot Head, Hampshire 1981. Complexity of design has certainly increased since then.

Crop circles are not a new phenomenon. Some believe they may have been part of the landscape since ancient times. A large proportion of crop patterns regularly appear in an area which has become known as the 'Wessex Triangle': its cardinal points are the areas around Silbury Hill, Warminster/Westbury and Winchester. The Triangle boasts the presence of England's largest stone circles, at Avebury and Stonehenge. The whole region is littered with burial mounds, many also circular. Silbury Hill is the largest man-made earthwork in Neolithic Europe. Considering the grandeur and sheer number of these ancient circular constructions, some have postulated that awestruck Neolithic farmers may have seen crop circles thousands of years ago and built their temples to mark and commemorate them. It is interesting to note that there have been some curious connections between the geometrical placement of stone circles and the geometry found in agriglyphs.

Though it is clear there are far more crop circles today, and they have clearly evolved in complexity, some modern farmers recall having seen them in fields all their lives, as did their parents and grandparents. The circles weren't reported either through fear or superstition or because they were not felt to be anything beyond some unusual natural occurrence, perhaps simply the result of animals or wind. Birds such as crows and rooks were likely suspects, being a common sight in fields of mature cereal crops, where they gather in circles to feed on ripened seed heads.

This 'circular damage' might also have been thought to be the result of strange crop diseases, which the owner would certainly not want to talk about for fear of losing a buyer. However, there is evidence to show that before the 1900s circle damage might have been attributed to fairies, or even the Devil, as in the famous 1678 woodcut on page 5.

The first crop formations to attract the serious attention of the media were the three circles found at Cheesefoot Head, Hampshire, late July 1981. The centre circle measured 17 metres across, with the smaller ones measuring 8 metres each. Researchers had been studying single circles as early as the late 1970s, but with little interest from the press. Even after the Cheesefoot Head circles were found, there were still few reports up until the mid-1980s, but interest began to grow. Though many single circles continued to be found for a while, it didn't take long for doubles, triples and quintuplets to show up in fairly rapid succession. In 1988, more than 100 circles were reported. In 1989,

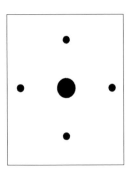

1988, Beckhampton, near Avebury, Wiltshire; a typical 'quintuplet'.

The Mowing - Devil :

Or, Strange NEWS out of

Hartford - ſhire.

Being a True Relation of a Farmer, who Bargaining
with a Poor Mower, about the Cutting down Three Half
Acres of Oats, upon the Mower's asking too much, the Far
mer ſwore, That the Devil ſhould Mow it, rather than He
And ſo it fell out, that that very Night, the Crop of Oat
Shew'd as if it had been all of a Flame; but next Morning
appear'd ſo neatly Mow'd by the Devil, or ſome Infernal Spi
rit, that no Mortal Man was able to do the like.
Alſo, How the ſaid Oats ly now in the Field, and the Owne
has not Power to fetch them away.

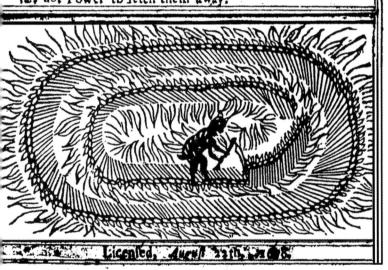

Licenſed, Auguſt 22th. 1678.

The Mowing Devil
This seventeenth-century pamphlet (front page seen here), issued in 1678 in Hertfordshire, England, appears to contain one of the earliest accounts of a crop circle. It tells of how a farmer discovered strange circles on his land after making flippant references to the Devil during a dispute with one of his workers. The circles were thus put down to being the work of the Devil himself.

The resemblance of the description and the accompanying illustration to what we would today recognise as at least a basic crop circle leaves many in no doubt that the Hertfordshire farmer was dealing with the same phenomenon still appearing today, albeit in more complex guises.

ie number had doubled to an annual average which has
:mained fairly steady since. The year of shock was 1990. The first
)ictograms', long chains of circles and rings combined with rec-
ngles and other shapes, appeared. In the years since, the ever-
ore elaborate and astonishing designs which have occurred have
ken the phenomenon to new heights and controversies which
o one could have guessed at in those early years (see 'The
volution of Crop Circles' on page 19).

Inside a Crop Circle

The lack of physical evidence in paranormal mysteries ha always been frustrating for researchers studying the Loc Ness monster, Bigfoot and UFOs. Quite the opposite occur when investigating crop circles. The evidence is there, in stunnin and beautiful form, for all to see.

With some notable exceptions, most crop circles appear to b created at night. Although it is possible they also form in less vi ble mediums at other times of the year (ice, snow, earth and gras rings have been reported), the vast majority are found betwee April and September in the Wessex area. Local weather condition do not seem to be a major factor in their arrival, despite some sug gestions to the contrary, as they are known to appear in rain an fog as well as clear conditions. They have been found on all type of soil worldwide, but the vast majority of English formations alig on what is known as aquiferous rock strata, which carries a lot c

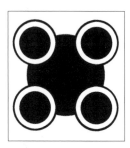

Headbourne Worthy, Hampshire, 7 July 1997.

water – such as the chalk of Wessex. Some believe this geological connection may be an important factor in their origins.

On nights crop circles arrive, there have occasionally been reports of buzzing electronic sounds, high-pitched whistling or loud roaring. Most notably, aerial light phenomena are often seen coming down into fields where new formations are subsequently discovered, and floating balls of light have been witnessed many times in and around existing patterns. Whether the circlemaking force comes from the sky, or emanates from the earth, or is a combination of both, isn't yet known, but eye-witnesses often speak of a descending presence.

Crop circles are known for their crisp, sharp edges, unusual design and flattened but largely undamaged stems. Though tractor lines cross most English fields, agriglyphs have also been found in the middle of fields without them, with no visible trails leading in. They are almost always fully within the selected field, although field boundaries have been crossed on noted occasions.

Entering a new formation is like opening a wonderful present. The circle wall will be clearly demarked from the rest of the crop, with little overspray of flattened stems into the surrounding area.

This close-up shows the distinctive swirled pattern of the floor of a crop circle. Notice the sharp edge between the floor and the wall of the formation.

Beckhampton, Wiltshire, 25 August 2002.

he plant stems will be flattened to the ground, flowing around xquisitely, almost with a fluid motion. Some circles are clockwise, ome anticlockwise, with no seeming preference. Radial lays have lso been known. Although the plants in the circle may be lying orizontally, they still grow without any apparent harm. Sometimes rop will recover, to stand straight again after a few days.

A variety of swirled centres can be found in crop formations, ome wide splays, others coned, rising like little tepees, and others ith a central standing tuft of crop. Often, it is hard to see what overall form the glyph has taken, since the patterns are best viewed from the air. All that can be seen on the ground are circles, paths and shapes of various sizes running off in every direction. Walking through a formation can have the exciting, mysterious and hypnotic quality of wandering through a maze or labyrinth.

Barbury Castle, Wiltshire, 23 July 1999.

Knoll Down, Wiltshire, 28 July 2002.

A representation of the Jewish Menorah and an accompanying glyph, at Barbury Castle, Wiltshire, 31 May 1999. This very sacred symbol in the fields was featured on the cover of the Jewish Chronicle.

People entering crop circles have reported experiencing a variety of physical and mental effects. Depending on the formation and on the individual, these can range from feelings of elation and peacefulness, to nausea, headaches, disorientation and panic. Some have reported feeling electrical tingles and other odd sensations. There have been notable cases of people's health seemingly being affected by the circles, whilst animals have been known to behave very strangely within them. Electronic equipment seems to malfunction way above the dictates of statistical chance, with mobile phone batteries draining and cameras failing. There have been several occasions where news crews have been frustrated when equipment has failed to work. Farmers have also reported combine harvesters breaking down when attempting to cut formations.

A number of causes have been put forward to account for these effects, including earth magnetism, unusual energy fields or even pesticides. So, a word of warning (especially if you neglect to ask the farmer's permission before entering the field!): Enter at your own risk!

Genuine or Hoax?

Tawsmead Copse, Alton Priors, Wiltshire, 9 August 1998.

12 June, 1995, Telegraph Hill, Cheesefoot Head, Winchester, Hampshire.

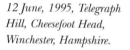

The greatest arguments over crop circles have concerned their origins – and whether they are the product of some unknown force or simply a man-made prank. Though uninformed opinion tends toward the latter, many others believe a significant proportion of formations demand a better explanation.

The layered, intricate and largely undamaged flow of crop inside many patterns is at odds with the human demonstrations carried out with planks and ropes over the years, which have often shown poor construction, footprints and dirt on stems, broken plants and holes in the ground where poles have been used as pivots. From a design point-of-view, a large number of crop patterns are perfectly formed, with sharp edges and a staggering geometrical precision, allowing accurate sacred numerical information and even astronomical data to be laid in the fields. The mathematics and geometry of crop formations have been the subject of whole books. Known man-made efforts fall down in comparison.

Beyond the rather unscientific, but not always unreliable method of simply sensing which formations feel right, there have been many attempts to determine hoaxed from genuine, but simple discernment and observation is often the most valuable tool. However, some have tried various detection techniques, including

Crop Circle Geometry

Diagrams revealing the ingenious and astonishingly accurate geometrical construction of three formations. All diagrams and geometrical analysis by Allan Brown, © 2003

 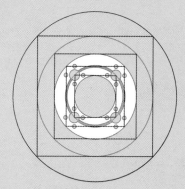

Telegraph Hill, Hampshire, 12 June 1995. The geometry of this formation is made up of four nested squares. The inner two squares define the positions of the large and small satellites.

Bishops Cannings, Wiltshire, 13 July 1997. This formation is made up from a series of pentagram relationships, with the centre defined by nested pentagons.

Etchilhampton, Wiltshire, 1 August 1997. A pentagram defines the outside edge of the inner ring. The ring is then used to define the curve of the 'rotating' arms, which then defines the inside edge of the formation's outer ring.

Pewsey, Wiltshire, 17 July 2002.

Opposite
*Avebury Trusloe,
Wiltshire, 2 June 2002.*

1e ancient art of dowsing, using rods and pendulums (see 'Theories and Beliefs'). A non-man-made crop circle will emit cer- tin kinds of energy in distinct patterns. Man-made pictograms roduce no results at all, according to some dowsers, though oth- rs have claimed the very act of making circles, at least in certain pecific areas, could actually change the energy patterns in the cale. The pattern of hoaxed sites appear to be different, however.

The most important thing to look at is the way the plants are id. In many formations all the plants are bent neatly to the round, and yet few are broken or dead. This is especially hard to ccomplish in rapeseed (canola), which snaps easily with the con- stency of celery, and yet has many times been found bent at 90 egree angles. Likewise, wheat-type stems are often found bent at 1e nodal joint to create certain shapes in the lay – an impossible at by manual handling.

How, then, are the stems bent? One theory is that the crop ircles are somehow heated. Exhaustive lab analysis into hundreds f crop circles carried out by biophysicist W. C. Levengood and 1e BLT Research team in the USA reveals unusual changes that ave taken place inside affected plants. Often the nodes have been lown open from the inside ('expulsion cavities'), which would ke a rapid and very brief rate of heating to accomplish. The seed avities and nodes are often elongated or mutated, and abnormal evelopments in the germination rate of the seeds have been oted.

Dowsing rods being used in a crop circle.

These results suggest the possibility that the plants have bee
exposed to short, intense bursts of microwave radiation. This ma
also explain those who display symptoms of negative effects afte
spending too much time in formations. No known man-made pa
terns have shown any strange biological changes, and yet th
majority of tested samples have shown these results.

Aside from physical effects, the many hours taken to creat
even fairly basic crop formations by human teams in publi
demonstrations throws heavy doubt on the notion that all pattern
are man-made. A significant number of designs have been know
to have appeared within very short periods of time, sometimes i
daylight hours, as at Stonehenge in 1996, where a 915 feet-lon
fractal pattern arrived within a 45 minute window in full view c
the A303 road at around 5.30 p.m., without being seen in the mak
ing (see picture on page 3). Sightings of aerial phenomena an
actual eye-witness accounts of circles forming also challenge th
total-hoax view (see 'Eye Witnesses and Sightings').

Of the known hoaxers there are, the first to claim authorshij
were a pair of elderly gentlemen named Doug Bower and Dav
Chorley who came forward in 1991. Doug and Dave achieved
certain amount of fame (or notoriety) when they claimed that th
whole thing started as a joke which had got out of hand. Thei

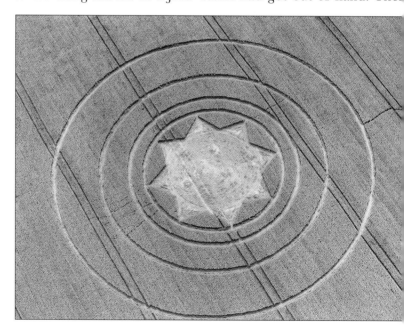

Avebury, Wiltshire, 11/12 August 1994.

orks were flattened using a plank held with a piece of rope, and
er with garden rollers. Evidence for any spectacular works was
otably absent, and their story failed to account for the large num-
rs of formations, nor explained the historical reports.

Other 'artists' have since come forward to claim they and their
nd make all crop circles, but in comparison to the more mysteri-
s designs, their demonstration works are without fail less
pressive and are rarely made within the same time and circum-
nces, with none of the unusual or intricate effects usually
served. Sometimes the attraction of working out how crop cir-
es could be made has become too great, and there have been
ses of serious researchers who have 'gone to the other side' and
come hoaxers themselves.

Given that most demo formations, often paid for handsomely
the media, are made by the same pool of three or four people,
e has to wonder where all the other mysterious artists are and
y they don't also try to capitalise on their craft.

Nevertheless, some of the human circlemakers there are say
at they feel they are creating sacred art. A few claim that while
ey make their formations, they feel they are being watched and
otected by a higher intelligence. Even Doug Bower claimed he
d Dave Chorley were being used by a higher power while they
re making the crop circles, but many feel this to be a sneaky
ystical smokescreen to blur the arguments.

Most accept that a proportion of crop glyphs are man-made,
t to say that ALL formations are man-made is to ignore the evi-
nce, much of which suggests something far stranger at work.

The Barbury Triangle
The glyph which appeared at Barbury Castle in 1991 featured triangle (or possibly a representation of a pyramid) with sides measuring about 60 yards, on top of which was a massive double-ringed circle. Situated a the points of the triangle were three circles, almost 30 yards across, and eac with a different design. Its three circles within a triangle evoke echoes of the power of three, the Triune, held in much respect by religion and especially practitioners o the arts of alchemy and sacred geometry. Indeed, it is strikingly similar to an illustration in a seventeenth century book on the Qabala (an ancient mystical belief), where it represents the Tree of Life, or the cosmi egg, in the process of creation. The glyph was situated in a place of power, and certain event that occurred close to the time of its creation, like loud roaring noise and strange lights in the sky, lent it an air of majesty.

The Evolution of Crop Circles

O ne of the most fascinating – and controversial – aspects of the circle mystery is how the patterns have changed and evolved over the years.

In the 1970s, the crop circles were largely just that – circles, whether single or in various combinations of clustered sizes. But from the end of the 1970s, and particularly in the early 1980s, patterns known as 'quintuplets' began to arrive, four small satellites round a central larger circle. As the 1980s progressed, rings developed, eventually combining with quintuplets to produce Celtic cross designs.

The years from the first 'pictograms' of 1990 saw the most significant development, and a big change occurred in the way the circles were viewed, for now they were unmistakable designs incorporating circles, arcs, rectangles, straight paths and beyond. Insect-like designs with curly features began to appear in 1991 and other 'animal' genres included a number of whale-like symbols. In the same year, one of the most spectacular pictograms ever seen appeared on 17 July in a field of wheat below the ancient hill-fort of Barbury Castle near Swindon, Wiltshire, being a triangular representation of a tetrahedron tipped with cryptic symbols at each point. It was by now clear that we were dealing with something of great sophistication, not simply some random weather phenomenon, as some had postulated.

A depiction of a 'Mandelbrot Set', the first truly recognisable design to appear, was found on 12 August 1991, at Ickleton, near Cambridge. Devised from the computer-driven science of 'fractals', self-replicating shapes creating infinite dimensions, a Mandelbrot Set is one of the most complex mathematical objects, used sometimes to demonstrate how order comes from chaos.

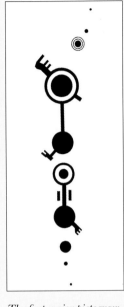

The first major pictogram, Alton Barnes, Wiltshire, 11 July 1990.

The Mandelbrot Set *Ickleton, Cambridgeshire, 12 August 1991. The first truly recognisable symbol to appear – a 'fractal' known as a 'Mandelbrot Set'.*

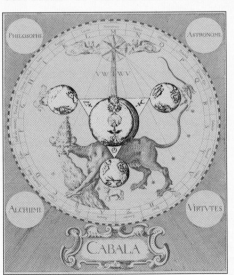

The engraving from the book Cabala, Speculum Altis et Naturae in Alchymia *published in 1654, bears a curious resemblance to the Barbury glyph on page 18.*

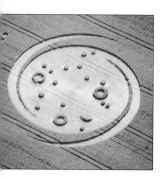

*West Stowell, Wiltshire,
23 July 1994.*

Were the makers of this formation asking us to consider the fine line between chaos and order? Was it a warning that if we continue our destructive ways, we could cross the line into chaos?

The representations of astronomical events were perhaps the most outstanding move forward. The aptly-named 'galaxy' design of 1994, for instance, were later found to be clear depictions of planetary alignment in the constellation Cetus, which would occur on 6/7 April 2000. When the predicted date finally arrived, one of the largest solar storms in years erupted, creating spectacular views of the aurora borealis across countries which normally wouldn't see it. Coincidence or prediction? 'Asteroid Belt' diagrams and clear depictions of our solar system, some showing the arrival of comets, and one (Longwood Warren, Hampshire, 1995) with the Earth mysteriously removed from the map, raised deep questions. These agriglyphs were unquestionably made with the impetus of some type of intelligence (see page 25).

*Longwood Warren,
Hampshire,
26 June 1995.*

In 1996 the return of fractal symbolism in ways that left the Mandelbrot Set looking simple by comparison. The 915 feet long Stonehenge formation of 7 July, which appeared by daylight (see 'Genuine o Hoaxed?'), was composed of 151 circles, and its amazing triple-armed successor at Windmill Hill (near Avebury) on 29 July took the number up to 194, with geometry that maintained 100% accuracy over an area many hundreds of feet across.

More fractal symbolism occurred in 1997 with the arrival of two 'Koch Snowflakes', huge decorative mandalas made up from small repeating triangles, bordered by fringes of tiny circles. By 2000, an extraordinary variety of designs were regularly visiting the fields and it seemed that any pattern one could think of could appear. In that year, hypnotic optical illusion-type formations of criss-crossing arcs staggered many with their breathtaking detail and accuracy.

In 2001 the largest crop circle to date appeared, when an 800 feet six-armed motif was discovered at Milk Hill, near Alton Barnes on 12 August. It contained within it a record-breaking 409 circle ranging from 70 feet across to just three feet across. The pattern arrived on a night of rain, the soil beneath the crop wet and slushy, yet it was found pristine and clean the next morning, with not a muddy footprint in sight. Television crews from around the world moved in on it with a great excitement not seen since the early 1990s.

However, the most dramatic development in the evolution of the symbolism came on 14 and 19 August 2001, when two clearly decipherable designs materialised next to the radio telescope complex at Chilbolton, Hampshire. One was an ingenious representation of a humanoid face, made up from differing-size pillars of crop, like pixels, whilst its companion was a rectangular strip which was a binary variation on a signal Mankind beamed out into space as a test transmission to hypothetical extra-terrestrials in 1974! Instead of information describing life on Earth, though, the Chilbolton version appeared to show details of life on another planet altogether!

The inevitable controversy and intense debate which followed these formations then deepened further in 2002 when another 'face and message' glyph came down at Crabwood, near Winchester, Hampshire on 15 August, a year and a day on from the first of the Chilbolton events. This huge and very cleverly constructed image (this time created with lines of variable width) clearly represented a classic 'grey' ET, holding out a disk containing binary code. When the message was found to be decodable into English computer text, it interpreted as (including text inconsistencies): "Beware the bearers of FALSE gifts & their BROKEN

Chilbolton, Hampshire, August 2001. A response to the nearby radio telescope? The pixellated face appeared 14 August, and the binary code on 19 August.

Crabwood, Sparsholt, Hampshire, 15 August 2002. This clear depiction of a 'classic' alien holding out an encoded disk generated shock and doubt in equal measure, but its construction is ingenious.

PROMISES. Much PAIN but still time. BELIEVE [presumably this word was damaged]. There is GOOD out there. We OPpos DECEPTION. Conduit CLOSING [a bell sound is signified]"

This formation both shocked and amused in equal measur leaving many to wonder what its true significance was, while sce tics and the now-dubbed 'believers' slugged it out.

Whatever, it was a demonstration of the clear progression the has been in the evolution of the shapes over the years - and y those which are truly identifiable are in the minority, while mo remain cryptic and open to personal interpretation. If the circl continue on, doubtless there will be yet more intriguing and imag native designs of a nature we haven't even dreamt about yet.

Hand in hand with the evolution of the shapes has been th development of the research community. Starting with just handful of dedicated investigators in the 1980s, by the 1990s

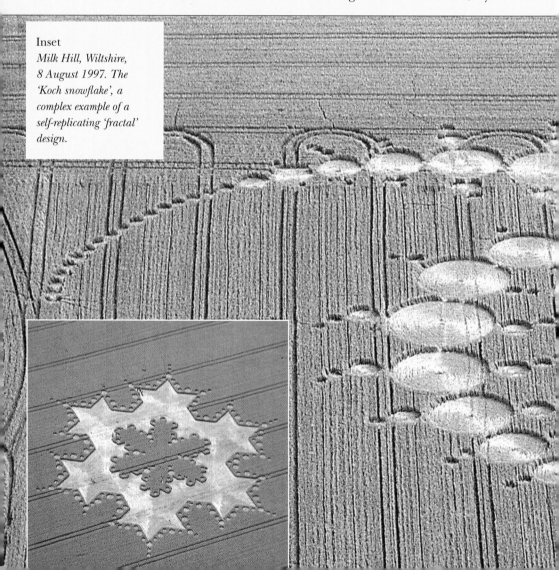

Inset
Milk Hill, Wiltshire, 8 August 1997. The 'Koch snowflake', a complex example of a self-replicating 'fractal' design.

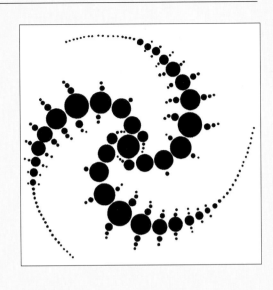

...indmill Hill, near
...ebury, Wiltshire,
... July 1996. Though
...ering many hundreds
... square feet, this triple-
...med fractal maintains
...0% accuracy in its
...ometrical layout. Still
...nsidered by many to be
...e of the best works of the
...enomenon.

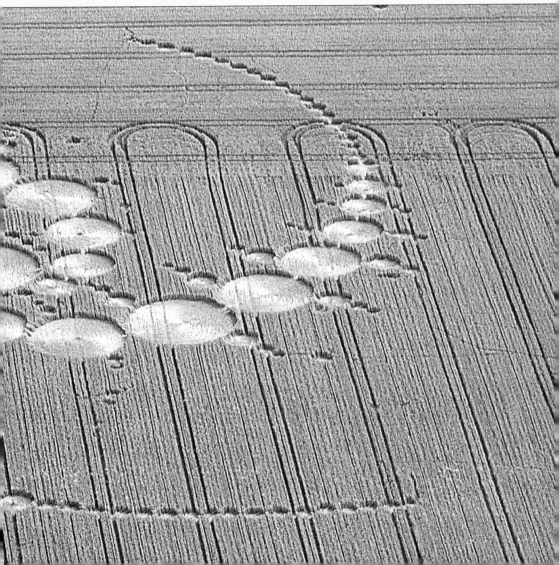

Milk Hill, Wiltshire, 12 August 2001. The largest formation yet recorded – 800 feet across, with 409 circles! (See page 20.)

whole industry of circle-tourists and enthusiasts had arisen, leading to a slew of journals and websites dedicated to the circle phenomenon. Inevitably, hoaxers and disinformation campaigns muddied the waters along the way, and bickering amongst the faithful flared up at times, but interest has remained high, despite all the debunking attempts. The extra interest stirred up by the arrival of Hollywood's (somewhat simplistic) take on crop circles, the Mel Gibson film *Signs* in 2002, created yet another generation of devotees, particularly in America where, for some, the circles were a new revelation, despite years of fantastic evolution and development in other parts of the world.

West Stowell, Wiltshire, 23 July 1994. This 'galaxy' design displayed an astronomical alignment due to take place on 6/7 April 2000!

Longwood Warren, Hampshire, 26 June 1995. A diagram of the earth's inner solar system – with only the earth missing.

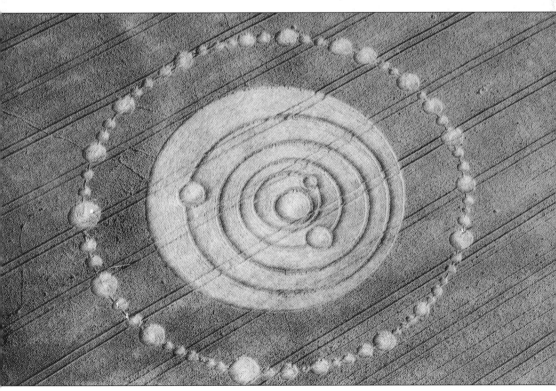

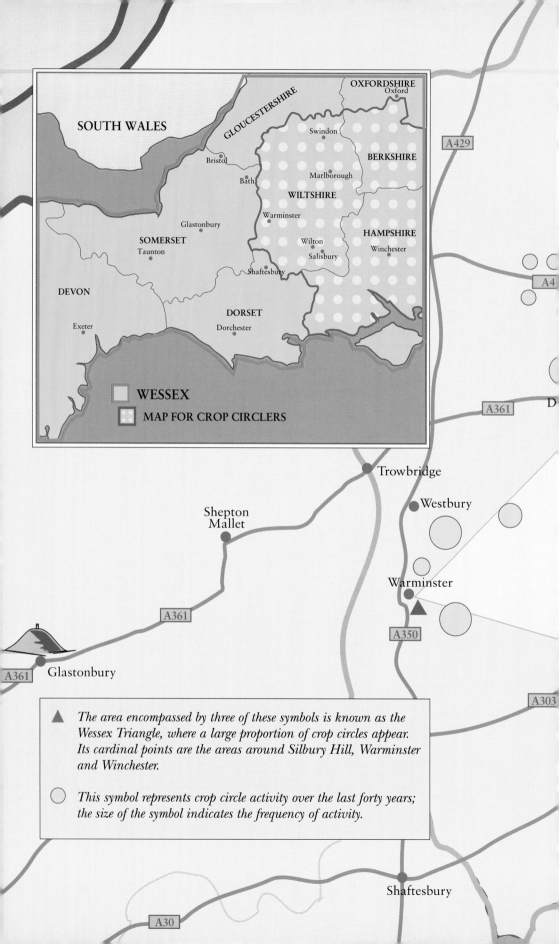

SOUTH WALES

GLOUCESTERSHIRE

OXFORDSHIRE
Oxford

Swindon

BERKSHIRE

Bristol

Bath

Marlborough

WILTSHIRE

Warminster

HAMPSHIRE

Wilton

Winchester

Salisbury

SOMERSET
Taunton

Glastonbury

Shaftesbury

DEVON

DORSET
Dorchester

Exeter

■ WESSEX

▦ MAP FOR CROP CIRCLERS

A429

A4

D

A361

Trowbridge

Westbury

Shepton
Mallet

Warminster

A361

A350

A361

Glastonbury

A303

Shaftesbury

A30

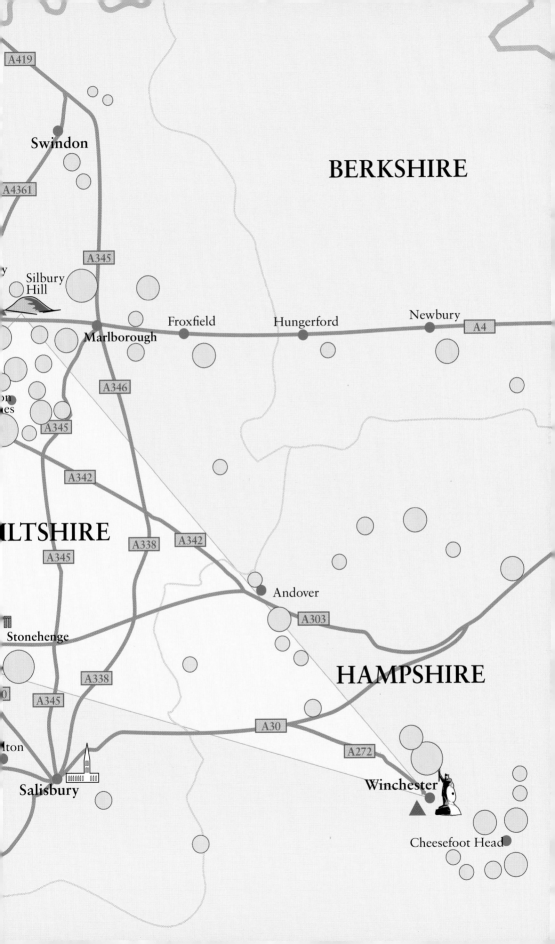

Crop Circle Development

*A selection of crop circle designs from the past to the present,
showing the evolution of sophistication.*

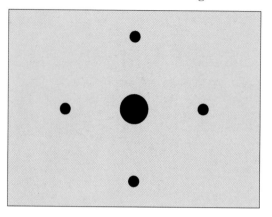

Silbury Hill, Wiltshire, 15 July 1988

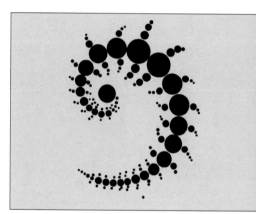

Sompting, West Sussex, 25 July 1990

Avebury, Wiltshire, 11/12 August 1994

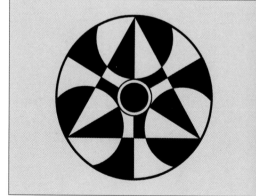

Stonehenge, Wiltshire, 7 July 1996

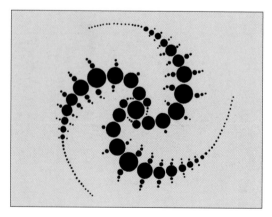

Windmill Hill, Wiltshire, 29 July 1996

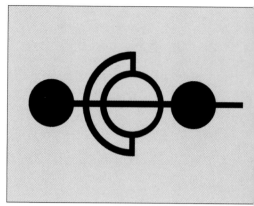

Winterbourne Bassett, Wiltshire, 1 June 1997

Milk Hill, Wiltshire, 8 August 1997

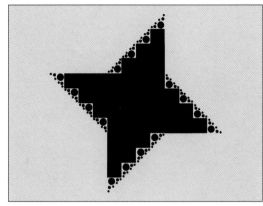

Silbury Hill, Wiltshire, 24 July 1999

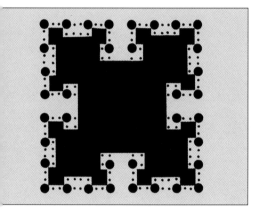

West Kennett, Wiltshire, 4 August 1999

Windmill Hill, Wiltshire, 14 July 2001

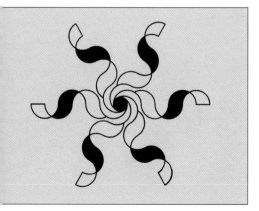

Stonehenge, Wiltshire, 4 July 2002

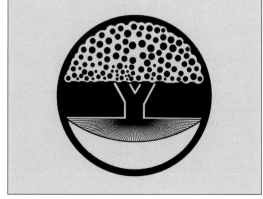

Alton Barnes, Wiltshire, 15 July 2002

Eye Witnesses and Sightings

Contrary to popular belief, there are around two dozen eye witness reports from people who have watched crop circles form in front of their eyes. One account tells of how the witness heard the crop emit a hissing sound, while the seed heads shook violently. Then, the plants fanned out into a circular shape on the ground. The entire process took just seconds. This occurred on a summer day without any clouds or wind.

Two more examples: In 1989, Vivienne and Gary Tomlinson claim a formation actually swirled around their feet as they were knocked from a path into standing crop by a force which took the form of 'mini-whirlwinds' funnelling down from the sky with a high-pitched whistling sound. In 2001, BLT Research co-ordinator Nancy Talbott became the first crop circle researcher to bear witness to an appearance, as she watched three tubes of light descend into a bean field at Hoeven, The Netherlands, leaving a steaming ellipse with an emanating pathway.

Though there are variations, as illustrated by these examples, in general there is a remarkable consistency to the eye-witness accounts, which convince many of the veracity of the reports. Sceptics insist all such eye-witnesses are liars, which is a pretty poor way to deal with things one can't handle.

Just one video exists which purports to show the appearance of a crop formation, allegedly taken at Oliver's Castle near Devizes, Wiltshire, in 1996. Lights are seen to circle over a field as a six armed snowflake design materialises beneath them. Great controversy still hangs over this footage, with many considering it faked with special effects. However, as yet, nothing has been proven for certain either way, despite claims and counter-claims.

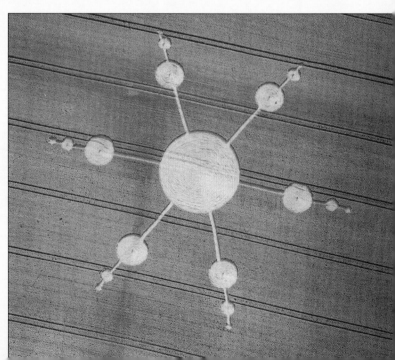

Strange lights in the sky have been known in England for centuries.
On 8 December 1733, a certain Mr Cracker of Fleet, Dorset saw *Something in the sky
which appeared in the north, but vanished from my sight, as it was intercepted by trees ...
On a sudden it re-appeared, darting in and out of my sight with an amazing coruscation.
The colour of this phenomenon was like burnished, or new washed silver. It shot with speed like
a star falling in the night. But it had a body much larger and a train longer than any
shooting star I have seen.*

Windmill Hill, Wiltshire,
2 August 2002.

The Sanctuary, Wiltshire,
18 August 2002.

Aside from direct sightings, night-time reports of aerial phenomena descending into fields where crop circles are subsequently found are the most common accounts. Some tell of clusters of lights, while other stories have included coloured columns of light shooting electric charges of some kind to the ground.

Other examples of bright lights seen in and around existing formations abound, and they have been filmed on a number of notable occasions. These lights are usually small, about the size of a beach ball, seen skimming over the seed heads, moving with uncanny precision in some cases, more randomly in others. Balls of light are considered so common around crop circles that some researchers casually refer to them as 'amber gamblers'.

Circle-related aerial phenomena can appear in many shapes beyond the usual small lights; cylinders, large spheres and even Ferris wheel-like objects have been seen. On occasion, lights have been seen to touch the ground softly, rise and float away – crop circles have been found at these sites the next day.

Certainly, what some would call UFOs have favoured the 'Wessex Triangle' region in the recent past. A major UFO 'flap' occurred around the Warminster area in Wiltshire during the 1970s, attracting international attention. The town even named itself 'UFO Capital of Europe'! Curiously, the phenomenon died down in the late 1970s and instead crop circles began appearing in the county.

The eminent psychologist Carl Jung wrote that anomalous lights in the sky were harbingers of great changes in the collective psyche, due to occur with the passing of the astrological Age of Pisces into the Age of Aquarius. He believed that the UFOs were actively involved in bringing about the changes. Though Jung saw UFOs more as projections of the mind, many believe the aerial lights and the increasing intricacy of the glyphs are an attempt by unidentified intelligent forces to communicate with us.

In addition to lights, unusual sounds have also been reported at crop circles. One in particular, a strange trilling noise that has been captured on tape, is the most common. Sceptics claim this sound is nothing more than a bird, but those who have heard it dispute this. Crackling, hissing and strange 'knockings' have also been noted.

As mentioned earlier in the book, circles often have physiological effects on visitors, ranging from feelings of elation, joy and mental clarity, to sensations of nausea, fatigue, metallic tastes in the mouth and disorientation. In certain instances, people claim

Golden Ball Hill, Wiltshire, 12 August 2001.

have been healed of physical complaints and injuries, at least temporarily. It seems to be a case of being in the right place at the right time – and in the right frame of mind. Some people can enter a formation and feel positive, whilst others may have a negative experience – perhaps the circles simply amplify the state one goes into the field with. These maladies could be caused by the 'energies' many believe are present in the formations, be they microwave or something more ethereal. Others point out that farmers spray fields with dangerous pesticides (not expecting the fields to be frequented by large groups of people) and this could be a factor in effects on health. However, crop circles do seem to emanate something beyond the physical, as the oft-reported effects on mechanical and electronic objects would suggest.

Alton Priors, Wiltshire,
22 July 2002.

Windmill Hill, Wiltshire
18 July 2002.

Theories and Beliefs

Biological factors have been suggested as the cause of at least simple crop circles. Many point to the well-known fairy rings as examples. However, there is no known fungi that n create the intricate crop lay and sophisticated patterns seen in me of the amazing pictograms. Lightning strikes and rare whirl- nds are other possibilities which have been put forward, but th tend to cause destruction, not the well-ordered results we see pictograms with their well-defined edges. Meteorologist Dr rence Meaden postulated a theory early on that a 'plasma vortex', electrically-charged funnel of air, might be responsible, but ough the idea did go some good way towards reaching for a ausible mechanism which might be behind the mystery, in its sic form it could only account for the simpler patterns, and the ding of very similar techniques at work in both the simple and e complex patterns left many questions unanswered.

'Cymatics', the effects of vibrations on physical media such as ter, oil and sand, has also been put forward as a possible factor. veloped in 1967 by Swiss scientist Hans Jenny, by transmitting und of various frequencies he was able to capture the exact geo- etric pattern of each frequency. Interestingly, as the complexity the frequencies rose, so too did the complexity of the cymatic apes, many of which bore remarkable resemblances to certain op circle patterns. Could crop circles be cymatic patterns left on e ground because of a rise in the vibrations of the earth? Many annellers and mediums, along with native people's prophecies, ve claimed that the earth is undergoing a change in its vibra- nary rate at this point in time. Most scientists agree that all mat- r is made of groups of vibrating particles. Since we are made of atter, we also vibrate at certain frequencies, and are affected by her vibrations. The rising complexity of the crop circles and ople's strong reactions to them may indicate an interaction tween ourselves and the changing vibrations of the planet.

Beckhampton, Wiltshire, 8 August 1999.

Earth Energies

Crooked Soley, Wiltshire,
27 August 2002 and
opposite.

Some say that crop circles are formed by a natural interactio from 'earth energies'. Increasingly there is a greater acceptanc of the theory that an invisible energy network covers the earth. has been suggested that quartz and underground water may pre duce this power source, as they are known to create piezoelectri fields under certain conditions. Underground water has lon been associated with the placement of crop circles – their obviou draw to aquiferous (water-holding) strata when circle distributio is mapped out onto geological maps is clear. Could this energy b helping to produce crop circles?

Some claim that this earth energy can be detected simpl through hands or bodies, but the ancient art of 'dowsing' is th most common method. The dowser holds a pair of rods, usuall made of bent wire (though twigs can also be used), or uses a per dulum. Walking slowly, he or she waits for the rods to start tur ing or the pendulum to twirl in a certain direction, indicating th a field of energy has been crossed. Some say that a force acts upo the rods, others insist that the energy affects the dowser, causin minute muscular twitches that can be felt and interpretec However, dowsing results can vary from person to person, whic has led to some criticism of the method.

Some types of earth energy apparently run in straight course These energy lines sometimes become confused with the concer of 'leys', alignments in the landscape which can most easily b seen by looking at maps and drawing a line through tumuli, buri mounds, churches and other old features in a join-the-dots fashio However, some postulate that ancient man placed their sacre sites on lines of earth energy, and hence leys may sometimes follo the same course as energy lines. Living in close proximity to th land, and dependent on it for their very lives, maybe thes Neolithic people could feel the power much more easily than w can today. This may also explain why crop circles, if utilising th same power source, cluster around so many areas of ancier sacred sites. There is evidence that these lines seem to act as magnet for light phenomena and other anomalous sighting (including, interestingly, ghosts). Crop circles often seem to for close to the nodal points of these bands of energy. The two ver powerful energy lines known as 'Michael and Mary' run direct through the Avebury area, the region of most crop circle activity.

However, despite the apparent plausibility of certain natur causes and earth energy theories, many formations clearly appe to display intelligent impetus: how can this be accounted for?

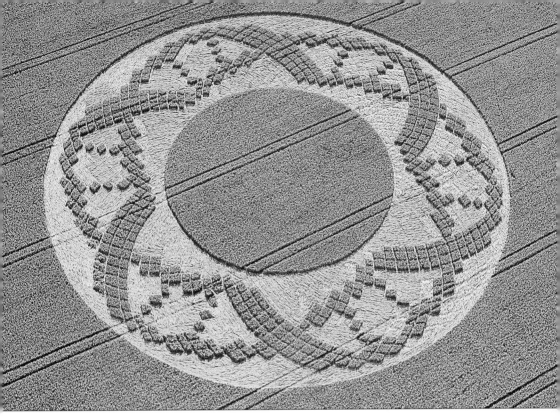

Many of the glyphs strongly suggest that the crop circles are trying to tell us something. Could they be a communication from higher beings, be they extra-terrestrial or from other dimensions (or even times)? The phenomenon has clearly evolved in complexity from year to year. Could this be a way of teaching language, starting slowly and simply, but gradually increasing the flow of symbolism and information?

There have been many cases of strange lights in the sky associated with crop circles, and these have often been interpreted as extra-terrestrial craft, though most seem too amorphous simply to be solid objects.

But if other beings were trying to communicate with us, why would they choose the medium of writing unintelligible graffiti in crop fields? And why not scatter them more evenly around the globe to attract general attention, not just in selected places? Although the theory offers more answers than some, it still leaves elusive logic holes to be covered.

If crop circles do carry some kind of intelligent message, as yet, no one has deciphered the overall code or meaning, despite a few recognisable symbols over the years. Could it be a language that isn't meant to be intellectually understood, but intuitively instead? Perhaps it is a language of vibration that we subconsciously understand deep within us. The strong reaction from some towards the symbolism would seem to suggest some truth to this.

Mathematically, the patterns certainly speak to us with a purity of geometry and form. It is possible that no one message is intended but that the glyphs are purely stimuli to encourage our race to greater aspiration and thought. The circles don't deliver answers but continually pose questions in a melange of multi-cultural, mathematical, astronomical – and totally obscure! – designs. It may be the very inspiration sparked in us to find an answer that could be their greatest gift, prodding us to expand and evolve without the need for direct celestial interference.

Human Consciousness

The crop circles (or the forces behind it) have on many occasions shown themselves to be responsive to human thought patterns. There have been cases of researchers hoping, privately, to see a certain type of design, only to find it the next day. Many have had premonitions and dreams of designs which arrive in reality later. On a number of notable occasions, controlled experiments with the power of the mind have managed to produce particular formations in the fields, seemingly projected from a group consciousness. Aerial phenomena have also been known to interact with observers, as if some kind of psychic link (as Carl Jung asserted) is involved.

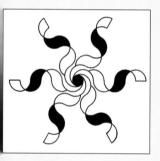

One possible solution to the mystery, therefore, may be that the crop formations are projections from the collective consciousness of humankind, somehow interacting with natural energy systems to produce shapes in the fields. This could partly explain the apparent randomness of the symbolism – a mish-mash of dream state feedback from the collective, intelligent on one level, yet uncoordinated. But what known mechanism exists in nature to allow for this – and how are patterns like the astronomical predictions to be accounted for? Like most theories, as many questions are raised by this idea as answers, but experiments show that human consciousness does at least appear to be one link in the chain of whatever creates the crop glyphs.

Gaia and Ancient Symbolism

Our earth itself may be creating the circles. The Gaia theory holds that the earth is a living, breathing organism, but New Age theory takes the notion a step further to credit our planet with active consciousness. Could the crop circles be the outward signs of where healing energy is being intelligently focused, a by-product given off as the earth tries to heal itself? They could be likened to sore spots, or welts, that can occur on a diseased organism, though their beauty suggests a more positive connotation. Some believe the circles are an actual premeditated attempt by Gaia to warn us that our destructive, polluting ways cannot be tolerated much nger before something drastic has to be done, a warning from e planet itself.

There is a view that the circles are ancient symbols which ppear here and there in history at times of need. Some Native mericans and other tribal groups have seen the crop glyphs as a ry from the earth, and a portent of coming great changes. A umber of groups around the world believe there is an imminent me of global transformation upon us and that the reappearance f these ancient patterns is to help raise our vibrational frequency, ven change our DNA, as certain formations which have displayed ear genetic symbolism might seem to suggest.

More than one formation has had strong echoes of the ncient Mayan culture, with some disturbing direct mathematical eferences to the numbers 2012 – the year, in western reckoning, n which the Mayan calendars end! Many cultures hold that 2012 ill be a time of great transformation – or destruction.

Stonehenge, Wiltshire, 4 July 2002. This formation was 750 feet in diameter, and was considered by many to be the most beautiful formation of 2002, placed perfectly within three round barrows.

The Military

Some have blamed the military for creating crop circles, citing the proximity of military land at Salisbury Plain to the circle sites of Wiltshire, and pointing to the many sightings of military helicopters over crop formations. What is missing in this possible explanation, however, is the nature of the technology involved (unknown) and what the motive might be. If it is for the testing of some new weapon or device, why demonstrate it in such public places when there are so many other secret locations that must be available? It has been suggested that the military might actively be looking for people's reactions to strange phenomena for some dubious purpose, but if so, why then invent so many hoaxers and debunkers to so successfully destroy interest in the subject?

There is evidence that the military are interested in the phenomenon, at least, and probably keep tabs on its development, hence, perhaps, the helicopter fly-overs witnessed so many times, though some have said it is just as likely crop formations simply make good ground markings to test pilots' flying abilities. Some have even suggested the downdraft from helicopter blades could account for crop circles, but comparing the mess left by helicopters which have come too low over formations, and the intricate beauty of the glyphs, leaves this theory as one of the least likely.

Unified Theory

The final answer to the mystery remains elusive after years of investigation. Maybe the solution lies in a combination of all these seemingly different ideas. Maybe an answer will never be found, or it lies so far beyond our current understanding and experience that we are simply not ready – nor expected – to comprehend the ultimate meaning or source. Perhaps it doesn't matter. The great beauty of the phenomenon is in its mystery as well as its complex designs. It may very well be the questions the crop circles spark which matter, not the answers. The inspiration and lines of enquiry which have been stimulated may be the all-important factors, and perhaps the greatest gift of all . . .

Alton Barnes, Wiltshire, 15 July 2002.

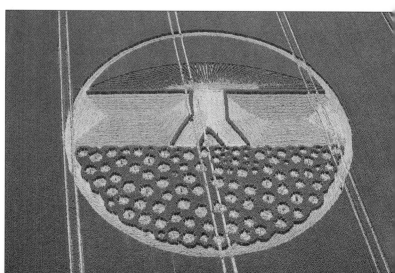

Epilogue

Many drawn to the crop circles have been profoundly affected by their influence. The questioning the phenomenon creates makes people look beyond the narrow confines of our society and its materialistic obsessions. Some have found themselves on a journey of spiritual self-discovery. Others have had mathematical or scientific revelations. Others still have become involved in psychic studies, healing and environmental concerns. The crop circles have opened doorways to new paths which might otherwise have remained closed to people without that first kick of the inner searching stirred by these beautiful and mysterious shapes.

Headbourne Worthy, Hampshire, 7 July 1997.

There has been a little disillusionment and even madness for some, too, for what phenomenon so challenging could produce only gentle nudges? The battle for reality between the 'believers' and debunkers has produced a platform for some astounding ideas and forced many to a position of confronting their deepest issues with the Universe. But the resulting investigation into the powers of the unseen – and perhaps unknowable – has created so much hitherto untapped energy through the lure of mystery, that we have everything to be grateful for. One thing is certain. Crop circles have the power to alter a person's life.

We still do not know who or what is making the agriglyphs. Our modern society, which bases 'truth' on science and empirical evidence, is always asking 'how'? Could it be that to find the answer, we should equally be asking 'why'? Why here? Why now? Is it because the human race now has the capacity to understand something new and far bigger than it has ever grasped before? Are we on the cusp of a new era for the planet and our race?

Regardless of what or who is making the stunning array of crop formations which bombard us each summer, they seem to strike a deep chord within us, alerting us to our need for the excitement of something new, outside of our normal experience. They have forced many people to re-think their view of the world. With the modern advances of science and technology and the problems they bring alongside their gifts, it is comforting for many to know there is still something unexplained and elusive out there to balance them, retaining a vital magic and mystery in our lives.

What the future will bring is anybody's guess. Each year people cry 'Nothing can surpass this!', and yet, each year, something does.

All that can be expected is the unexpected.

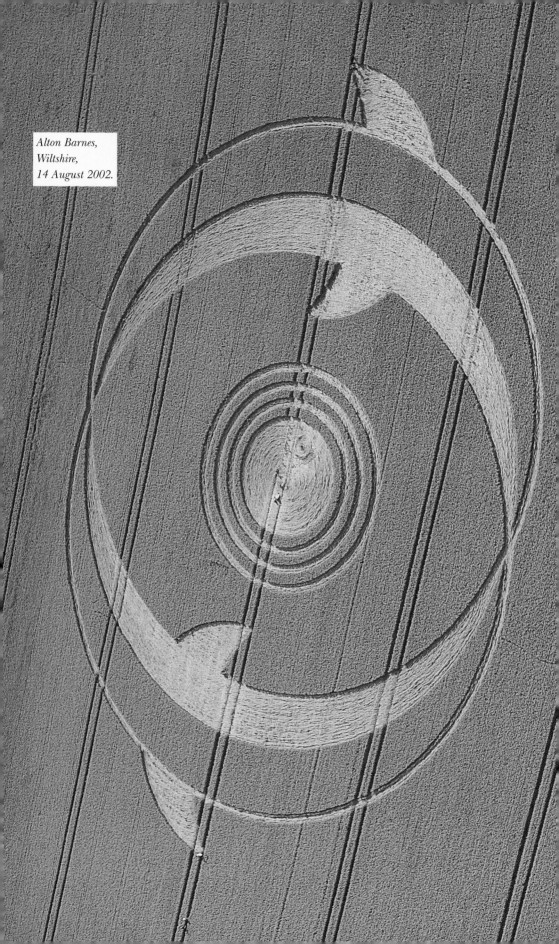

*Alton Barnes,
Wiltshire,
14 August 2002.*

Some Notable Crop Formations

August 1972. Starr Hill, Warminster, Wilts. Circles/angles allegedly seen forming.
ummer 1975. Stonehenge, Wilts. Triangular triplet.
ummer 1978. Headbourne Worthy, Hants. First official uintuplet.
ummer 1978. Cheesefoot Head, Hants. Symmetrical plet.
y 1981. Cheesefoot Head, Hants. Further symmetrical plet, reported in media.
July 1984. Alfriston, E. Sussex. Quintuplet otographed by Denis Healey MP.
July 1986. Cheesefoot Head, Hants. Three ringed rcles.
August 1986. Longwood Estate, Hants. First official ltic Cross.
June 1987. Whiteparish, Wilts. Ringed circle w/path-y.
July 1987. Cheesefoot Head, Hants. Quintuplet, first ficial radial lay.
June 1988. Corhampton, Hants. Triangular triplet spoked lay.
y 1988. Silbury Hill, Wilts. Two quintuplets w/circles.
August 1989. Winterbourne Stoke, Wilts. Circle quartered lay.

90

May. Chilcomb, Hants. First official pictogram. First oxes'.
June. Longwood Estate, Hants. Circle with broken gs.
June. Chilcomb, Hants. Triple-haloed dumb-bell.
ne-July. Bishops Cannings, Wilts. Two Celtic Crosses, e superimposed.
July. Alton Barnes, Wilts. Much-publicised pictogram 'claws'.
July. Stanton St Bernard, Wilts. Pictogram w/ aws'.
July. Crawley Down, Wilts. 'Boxed' pictogram.
July. Beckhampton, Wilts. 'Scrolls' & triangles.
July. East Kennett, Wilts. Pictogram w/ 'claws'.
August. Cheesefoot Head, Hants. Two pictograms, one ge, one small.

1991

7 July. Alton Barnes, Wilts. Long pictogram.
10 July. Stonehenge, Wilts. 'Insectogram' & ringed circle.
17 July. Barbury Castle, Wilts. Complex triangular pictogram.
19 July. Alton Priors, Wilts. Slanted 'key' pictogram.
27 July. East Kennett, Wilts. Straight 'key' pictogram.
August. Milk Hill, Wilts. Hieroglyphic script.
1 August. Beckhampton, Wilts. Best of several 1991 'whales'.
12 August. Ickleton, Cambs. 'Mandelbrot Set' fractal.
15 August. Manton, Wilts. Clear video of light ball taken in pictogram.
18 August. Froxfield, Wilts. 'Serpent' or 'Brain'.

1992

9 July. Alton Barnes, Wilts. 'Snail' pictogram.
16 July. Milk Hill, Wilts. Circles & curved paths.
24 July. East Meon, Hants. Haloed pictogram.
24 July. Oliver's Castle, Wilts. Triangular triplet formed in response to meditation.
2 August. West Stowell, Wilts. Mercury astrological symbol.
9 August. Froxfield, Wilts. Long pictogram.
12 August. Alton Priors, Wilts. Ringed crescent.
16 August. Silbury Hill, Wilts. 'Charm Bracelet' ring.

1993

7 July. Charley Knoll, Loughborough, Leics. Complex cruciform pictogram.
11 July. East Kennett, Wilts. Ring encircling T-junction.
11 July. West Kennett, Wilts. 'Nautilus' & zigzag.
11 July. West Overton, Wilts. '666' emblem.
7 August. Cherhill, Wilts. 'Hands of Friendship' pictogram.
4 September. Bythorn, Cambs. 10-petalled mandala.

1994

7 July. Barbury Castle, Wilts. Crescents/circles 'insect'.
15 July. Bishops Cannings, Wilts. 'Scorpion'.

23 July. West Stowell, Wilts. 'Galaxy' star map. Best of three similar 1994 designs.

23-24 July. East Dean, W. Sussex. Two 'thought bubble' designs.

26 July. Ashbury, Oxon. Quarter-mile-long pictogram.

27 July. Oliver's Castle, Wilts. Nested crescents.

28 July. West Overton, Wilts. 'Infinity' symbol.

4 August. Froxfield, Wilts. 'Flower of Life'.

11/12 August. Avebury, Wilts. 'Web/dreamcatcher' emblem.

14 August. Avebury Trusloe, Wilts. 'Curled scorpion'.

1995

29 May. Beckhampton, Wilts. Spiral.

31 May. Alfriston, E. Sussex. 4-armed 'Catherine wheel'.

12 June. Telegraph Hill, Chilcomb, Hants. Quintuplet of quintuplets w/'aum' symbol.

20 June. Bishops Sutton, Hants. 'Asteroid belt'.

26 June. Longwood Estate, Hants. Solar system ('Earth missing') diagram.

29 June. Felbridge, W. Sussex. Rings & circles formed in response to meditation.

Mid-July. East Meon, Hants. Nested crescents.

6 July. Dunley, Hants. Multi-rings & 'intestine'.

7 July. Long Marston, Warwicks. 'Eye' emblem.

15 July. Cissbury Ring, W. Sussex. 'Time tunnel' rings.

23 July. Winterbourne Bassett, Wilts. Ringed squares.

1996

17 June. Alton Barnes, Wilts. 'DNA' double helix.

7 July. Stonehenge, Wilts. 'Julia Set' fractal, formed by day.

12 July. Littlebury Green, Essex. 6-petalled 'flower'.

26 July. Ashbury, Oxon. Vesica Pisces.

29 July. Etchilhampton, Wilts. 4100ft paths & circles.

29 July. Windmill Hill, Beckhampton, Wilts. Triple 'Julia Set' fractal.

Early August. Streatley, Barton-Le-Clay, Beds. Circles & semi-rings.

2 August. Liddington Castle, Wilts. 'Brooch' emblem & fractal.

11 August. Oliver's Castle, Wilts. 6-armed 'snowflake'. Claimed videoed forming.

1997

20 April. Barbury Castle, Wilts. 6-petalled flower.

4 May. Burderop Down, Wilts. Qabalah/'Tree of Life'.

1 June. Winterbourne Bassett, Wilts. 'Chinese puzzle'.

9 June. Stonehenge, Wilts. Hexagonal 'snowflake'.

11 July. Alton Barnes, Wilts. 'Torus knot'.

14 July. Cley Hill, Wilts. Spoked hexagon.

23 July. Silbury Hill, Wilts. 'Koch Snowflake' fractal.

1 August. Etchilhampton, Wilts. 6-armed star & 780-box grid.

8 August. Milk Hill, Wilts. 'Koch Snowflake' fractal.

18 August. Hackpen Hill, Wilts. 'Strange Attractor' fractal.

1998

3 May. West Kennett, Wilts. 'Beltane Wheel'.

19 June. Clanfield, Hants. Clustered rings & semi-circles

20 June. Beckhampton, Wilts. 10 petals encircling pentagram

4 July. Dadford, Bucks. Double pentagram w/'bird', ankh & 'Ganesha' symbols.

5 July. Danebury Ring, Hants. 7-petalled ring.

9 July. Alton Barnes, Wilts. 7-petalled mandala.

11 July. Lockeridge, Wilts. 'Dragon/bug'.

21 July. Beckhampton, Wilts. 'Manta Ray'.

7 August. Lockeridge, Wilts. 'Insect Queen'.

8 August. Beckhampton, Wilts. Double pentagram on pentagon.

9 August. Tawsmead Copse, West Stowell, Wilts. 7-sided mandala.

1999

2 May. Middle Wallop, Hants. Eclipse sequence.

23 May. Avebury Trusloe, Wilts. 'Biology' symbol.

31 May. Barbury Castle, Wilts. Hebrew Menorah.

12 June. Alton Barnes, Wilts. Multi-pictogram.

4 July. Hackpen Hill, Wilts. Triple-armed complex swirl.

16 July. Windmill Hill, Beckhampton, Wilts. Square of 288 circles.

18 July. Cherhill, Wilts. 9-pointed mandala.

19 July. Devil's Den, Wilts. Complex star on hexagon.

28 July. Beckhampton, Wilts. 3-D 'ribbon' emblem.

31 July. Roundway, Wilts. 14-armed star.

6 August. Bishops Cannings, Wilts. 7-armed 'basket weave' star.

June. Windmill Hill, Wilts. 3-D chequer board.
July. East Kennett, Wilts. 1600-componented grid.
July. Bishops Sutton, Hants. Clustered rings &
mi-circles.
July. Everleigh Ashes, Wilts. Celtic cross encircling
rrow.
July. Avebury Trusloe, Wilts. 'Magnetic fields'
andala.
July. Silbury Hill, Wilts. 6 pentagrams, one 'broken'.
July. Uffington, Oxon. Pictogram below white horse.
August. Chilbolton, Hants. Ring cluster by radio
escope.
August. Picked Hill, Wilts. 'Sunflower' of 44 arcs.

01

June. Wakerley Woods, Northants. Mayan calendar
heel.
June. Berwick Bassett, Wilts. Curved triangle cluster.
June. Badbury, Wilts. 'Oroborous' (coiled Mayan
ake).
June. Alton Barnes, Wilts. 'Pyramid' with sun rays.
-13 July. Great Shelford, Cambs. Growing ring, maze
square mandala.
July. Great Shelford, Cambs. 'Angel' of radiating
es.
July. Lockeridge, Wilts. Radiating mandala.
August. Milk Hill, Wilts. Record-breaking 800ft
armed spiral, 409 circles!
-19 August. Chilbolton, Hants. 'Face' & 'message' by
dio telescope.
August. Hoeven, The Netherlands. Ellipse w/path,
tnessed forming by Nancy Talbott of BLT Research.

02

June. Avebury Trusloe, Wilts. 'Celtic knot'.
June. Sompting, West Sussex. White silica dust found
rinkled in pictogram.
June. West Overton, Wilts. Double-headed spiral.
July. Stonehenge, Wilts. 750ft 6-armed 3-D 'ribbons'.

15 July. Alton Barnes, Wilts. 'Apple tree' emblem.
17 July. Pewsey, Wilts. 'Nautilus shell'.
18 July. Windmill Hill, Wilts. Complex criss-crossed
mandala.
22 July. Alton Priors, Wilts. Square 'knotted' mandala.
28 July. Knoll Down, Wilts. 76-segmented 'church
window'.
14 August. Alton Barnes, Wilts. 'Dolphins' motif.
15 August. Crabwood, Sparsholt, Nr Winchester, Hants.
Alien face & coded disc.
27 August. Crooked Soley, Wilts. 'DNA' ring.
September. Kew Gardens, London. Flower design
formed in secure walled area!

*The above list is of some circular highlights
of the last thirty years selected by Andy Thomas.
The circles are arranged chronologically.
See map on pages 26/27 in conjunction with this.*

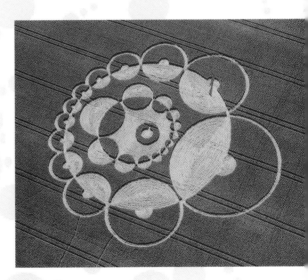

*Bishops Sutton,
Hampshire, 14 July
2000.*

Further Information

Selected Reading (A-Z by authors)

Crop Circle Year Books, Steve Alexander & Karen Douglas, Temporary Temple Press 1999 onward 28pp

Crop Circles: Exploring the Designs & Mysteries, Werner Anderhub & Hans Peter Roth, Lark Books, 2002, 144pp

Crop Circles: Harbingers of World Change, ed. Alick Bartholomew, Gateway 1991, 192pp

Ciphers in the Crops, ed. Beth Davis, Gateway 1992, 88pp

Circular Evidence, Pat Delgado & Colin Andrews, Bloomsbury 1989, 190pp

Crop Circles, Michael Glickman, Wooden Books 2000, 58pp

The Deepening Complexity of Crop Circles, Dr Eltjo Haselhoff, Frog Ltd. 2001, 157pp

The Cosmic Connection, Michael Hesemann, Gateway 1996, 168pp

Mysterious Lights and Crop Circles, Linda Moulton Howe, Paper Chase Press 2000, 342pp

Crop Circles: The Hidden Form, Nick Kollerstrom, Wessex Books 2002, 64pp

Crop Circle Geometry, John Martineau, Wooden Books 1992 onwards, varied pages

The Circles Effect and its Mysteries, George Terence Meaden, Artetech 1989, 116pp

The Face & the Message, John Michell, Gothic Image 2002, 36pp

Crop Circles Revealed, Judith Moore and Barbara Lamb, Light Technology Publishing 2001, 265pp

The Crop Circle Enigma, ed. Ralph Noyes, Gateway 1990, 192pp

Crop Circles: The Greatest Mystery of Modern Times, Lucy Pringle, Thorsons 1999, 144pp

Crop Circles: A Mystery Solved, Jenny Randles & Paul Fuller, Robert Hale 1990, 250pp

Round in Circles, Jim Schnabel, Penguin 1993, 295pp

Secrets in the Fields, Freddy Silva, Hampton Roads 2002, 334pp

Fields of Mystery, Andy Thomas, S B Publications 1996, 100pp

Quest for Contact, Andy Thomas & Paul Bura, S B Publications 1997, 144pp

Vital Signs: A Complete Guide to the Crop Circle Mystery and Why it is NOT a Hoax, Andy Thomas, S B Publications (Frog Ltd in USA) 1998, revised 2002, 192pp

The Secret History of Crop Circles, Terry Wilson, CCCS 1998, 155pp

Crop Circle Journals

THE CIRCULAR REVIEW: Post Restante, Royal Mail Delivery Office, North Street, Pewsey, Wiltshire SN9 6EU, UK

MEDWAY CROP CIRCULAR: Medway Crop Circle, 87 Hurstwood, Chatham, Kent, ME5 0XH, UK

THE SPIRAL: Wiltshire Crop Circle Study Group, PO Box 2079, Devizes, Wiltshire, SN10 1US, UK

Selected Websites

SWIRLED NEWS http://www.swirlednews.com

CROP CIRCLE CONNECTOR http://www.cropcircleconnector.com

BLT RESEARCH http://www.bltresearch.com

TEMPORARY TEMPLES http://www.temporarytemples.co.uk

GLASTONBURY SYMPOSIUM http://www.glastonburysymposium.co.uk

INVISIBLE CIRCLE http://invisiblecircle.de/uk

West Overton, Wiltshire, 23 June 2002.

About the Editor

ANDY THOMAS is a leading crop circle researcher and author of three books exploring aspects of the phenomenon: *Fields Of Mystery*, *Quest For Contact* (with Paul Bura), and the widely referenced *Vital Signs*, described by many as the definitive guide to crop circles.

Andy is a founder member of the Southern Circular Research team and is editor of the influential web site **www.swirlednews.com** (for information on this and other titles by Andy Thomas, see **www.vitalsignspublishing.co.uk**). Before that he edited the long running crop circle journal *SC* for nine years. He is also author of two books about his historical home town of Lewes in East Sussex, *Streets of Fire* and *The Lewes Flood*.

Andy writes and lectures widely in England and abroad, and has made numerous radio and TV appearances. UK spots have included Channel 4's *Richard and Judy* show, BBC 2's *Esther*, and ITV's GMTV *Breakfast Show*. Andy has also featured in many programmes from the USA, Japan, Germany, Italy and other countries.

Acknowledgements

All photographs in this book have been taken by Steven Alexander except for the following for which the publishers gratefully thank:

Alexander Grenfell p.2;
Jürgen Krönig pp. 7 inset, 18;
Busty Taylor pp. 10 top, 12, 16, 17, 22 (x2), 24, 31, 41;
Richard Wintle pp. 7, 11.

This book is based on an original text by Kent Goodman entitled *Crop Circles – an Introduction*. Revised, enlarged and edited by Andy Thomas.

All diagrams are © Allan Brown, 2003

Cover illustration by Andrew Jamieson.

Cover design, typesetting, layout and map by Alexander S. Grenfell.

Published by Wessex Books 2003. Reprinted 2006.

Text © Andy Thomas, based on an original by Kent Goodman.

Design © Wessex Books 2003

Printed in India

ISBN 1-903035-17-1